Inbox Outbox Unbox NOBOX
Four Steps to Delete Your Box Thinking

Holly Porter

**TRANSFORM
PUBLISHING**

Inbox Outbox Unbox NOBOX
Four Steps to Delete Your Box Thinking
Copyright © 2017 by Holly Porter. All Rights Reserved.

Published by: Transform Publishing
Info@TransformMastermind.com
(567) 259-6454

ISBN: 978-0-692-91975-0
Library of Congress: 2017911296
Editor: Elena Rahrig
Printed in the United States of America
First Edition

DEDICATION

This book is dedicated to my Husband, Scott Porter. He has always been my loudest cheerleader. He listens to my rants and often flowing crazy ideas, along with being my rock during my times of seemingly falling apart. He is my best friend and who I am happy to wake up next to each morning. I appreciate all his hard work as a husband, father, and provider to eight children.

INTRODUCTION

"I don't think inside the box.
I don't think outside the box.
I don't even know where the box is!"

In my mind, I found myself often saying: *"Step away from the box and get rid of the box. Don't limit what you can do by boxing yourself in."* Compared to the masses, I have always been a different type of thinker when it comes to life. I know there is typically a better (or more unique), way to get things done.

The word (my word), is *Figureoutable*...which means...everything can be figured out. I whole-heartedly believe, and know, everything is figureoutable. When you limit yourself to what is truly possible, you are in, what I call, Box-Thinking mode. In this book, you will be coached, not only on how to get out of your box, but on how to get rid of your box altogether.

> "Many people will only love you
> as-long-as you fit into their box.
> Don't be afraid to disappoint them!"

How do you think it would feel to have NOBOX? I encourage you (if you must), to kick, stomp, and/or step away, to change your thinking—change your mindset—so you have NOBOX. Simply put, "Do whatever it takes!"

"Instead of thinking outside the box, get rid of the box."

This book has been on my mind for a few years, and it was only recently when I realized exactly what it would look like, how it would be articulated, and how it would reach you. I know, without a shadow-of-a-doubt, for this book to accomplish what it was created for, it must include the following four attributes:

1. FUN

I am guessing you are like most, in that you love to be entertained. Am I correct? This is exactly why I have structured this book in a way that allows you to enjoy the process of getting UNBOXED; all the while, feeling and knowing that you are part of the process through relation and visualization of the lessons within this book.

2. ADVENTUROUS

As you read and learn more about which shoe persona you are, you will feel my presence as I take this adventure with you. Along your adventure, be sure to give thought to why you do what you do and what motivates you to succeed in both life and business.

3. REALISTIC

Goals. Goals. Goals. Ever-flowing goals. Ideas are everywhere and quickly turn into goals. Before you know it (if you are none-the-wiser), you find yourself with goals and deadlines impossible to achieve—not seemingly impossible; rather, truly impossible. More than likely, you have set goals that send you on a rocky road to please everyone who surrounds you. As you take your adventure through this book, please keep at the forefront of your mind, you cannot be everything to everyone and it's okay to just BE YOU. Know that, "You are ENOUGH."

4. EDUCATE

For years I have studied personalities and what makes people tick—what makes them who they are and do what they do. I may not be the end-all expert or shoe expert in personalities; however, the shoe personas remind me of the movie, *What Women Want*, starring Mel Gibson. Knowing what I know, I'm not sure Mel Gibson ever truly figured out what it is that women want. (Of course, not from lack of trying.) Truth is, women can be a challenge to figure out sometimes. Perhaps it is the one thing that isn't figureoutable…well, to men at least. This is only my opinion. It's is a good thing some men like challenges.

With that being said, answer this: Are you an introvert or an extrovert? Yin or Yang Energy? Do you know what that even means? If not, would you like too? Before you take the shoe persona test in this book, you will see a short description of Yin and Yang Energy, and Fire, Air, Earth, and Water Elements. This way, you will better understand your test results.

One thing I want you to remember as you read this book is, this book is designed to be fun for you. So, be sure not to get caught up worrying if your shoe persona is far different from your friends. Know that, we can all learn from each other. Even more, remember the importance of loving others for who they are and loving yourself for who you are. In all reality, we all march to the beat of our own drum. Some tunes are louder and we can hear them coming from a mile away; while other tunes, you can barely hear at all. However, whatever beat you march to, know it fits perfectly with who you are—never apologize for it. So, let your hair down, put your big girl panties on, and let's play!

"It's not about the shoes,
it's about
what you do with them."
—Michael Jordan

Yin and Yang Definitions

Yin Yang is widely known as the two opposites that complete the whole. According to a Chinese theory, there are two forces in the universe in which energy divides and whose fusion in physical matter brings the phenomenal world into being.

Yin is the passive feminine energy. Water is a Yin Energy, and its passive nature allows you to easily move your hand through it. Yin Energy accepts and gives over to its surrounding energy. Earth is also Yin Energy. When Yang Energy is added to Yin Energy, it becomes either a creative or destructive element. The nature of passivity appears to be weak, but its strength comes in its ability to transcend other energies.

Yang is the active masculine energy. According to this theory, wise people will detect these forces in the seasons, in their food, and so on; then they will regulate their lives accordingly. Yang energy is aggressive. The power of Yang Energy is what drives creativity. Passion and fire fuel Yang Energy. Fire and air are Yang elements.

The Element of Fire

Positive Qualities: decisiveness, vigorousness, zeal, enthusiasm, courage, decisiveness, power of creativity, daring, sedulity

Negative Qualities: quarrelsomeness, irritability, urge to destroy everything, passion, immoderacy, jealousy, voraciousness, vindictiveness, violence, hate, anger, sudden ebullition

The Element of Air

Positive Qualities: vigilance, Care-free, kind-hearted, optimism, trusting nature, clarity, lightness, independent, dexterity, diligence, smiler, joy, acuity

Negative Qualities: dishonesty, lack of perseverance, dishonesty, gossipy, backbiting, cunningness, garrulousness, touchiness, inconstancy, prodigality

The Element of Water

Positive Qualities: mildness, possessiveness, understanding, placidity, trusting, devotion, forgiveness, mercy, compassion, modesty, fervor, pliancy, meditativeness, internalization

Negative Qualities: heartlessness, indifference, laziness, indolence, lack of daring, rigidity, unstableness, dejection

The Element of Earth

Positive Qualities: conscientiousness, consistency, punctuality, resistance, caution, responsibility, firmness, carefulness, reliability, ambition, sobriety, respectfulness, matter-of-factness

Negative Qualities: superficially, laziness, stuffiness, indifference, cumbersomeness, lack of conscientiousness, touchiness, irregularity, timidity, scornfulness

Personality is the core thoughts and feelings inside of you that tell you how to conduct yourself. It's a checklist of responses, based on strongly held values and beliefs. It directs you to respond emotionally or rationally to every life experience. Your personality even determines how you react to others. It is an active process within you that manages how you feel, think, and behave. Knowing more about yourself and others, is vital to your success. Your core personality can never be changed—it is yours forever! You can however, develop skills in other personality personas. Next, I will guide you through a shoe test to help you discover your shoe persona—your personality.

"Successful women can still have their feet on the ground, they just wear better shoes."

IF YOU WERE A SHOE, WHAT KIND OF SHOE WOULD YOU BE?

On the next page is a simple test to see where your personality fits in the world of shoes. Answer the questions as your younger-self, as it seems to be the truest conclusion. Remember, your first answer is usually the best and truest answer. Do not over think it...just have fun! (This is not meant to frustrate you.)

I kept it to four basic personas; but, remember, there is NOBOX. You can be natural and become anything you desire to become. Just like there are many styles, brands, and colors of shoes, there are also many styles, brands, and colors of people—no two people are exactly alike.

Inbox Outbox Unbox NOBOX

Alright, let's begin!

1. If you had $5,000 to go anywhere in the world, where would you go?

   A. Fiji
   B. On a fantastic eco-tour in Costa Rica
   C. On a fast tour to Eastern Europe
   D. To an elite spa somewhere far away

2. When you're living your best, you seek:

   A. Action and adventure
   B. Purpose and security
   C. Play and excitement
   D. Safety and acceptance

3. How would you describe your bedroom?

   A. Perfectly decorated and neat
   B. Decorated with hand me downs, cozy, and laid back
   C. Decorated with fun prints and expressions
   D. Simple, clean, and organized

4. If you were in a member's club, what would you be?

   A. Of course, the President
   B. The Secretary. I'm good at staying organized.
   C. The party planner…it's all about the party!
   D. The Vice President. I can help when needed; but, I don't have to be in charge.

5. You just found a $100 bill in one of your coat pockets. What would you do with it? (First reaction.)

   A. Donate it to a non-profit organization.
   B. Use the money to have your coat dry-cleaned.
   C. Treat yourself and your significant other to a concert to see your favorite band.
   D. Buy new shoes or cute bag you've had your eye on.

6. It is time to clean out your closet. What's one item you would never part with?

   A. The leather jacket with zippers
   B. The cashmere sweater your mom gave you
   C. The favorite pair of worn-in jeans
   D. The pencil skirt that makes your legs look really great

7. What is your favorite ice cream?

   A. Strawberry
   B. Chocolate
   C. Banana Split
   D. French Vanilla

8. How would your best friend describe you?

   A. Cutting-edge
   B. Reliable
   C. A barrel of laughs
   D. Socially conscious

9. You've got a three-day weekend coming up, what are your plans?

   A. Sticking to a regular routine
   B. Organizing your room/house
   C. Hanging out with friends
   D. Work on your artistic skills

10. You've become good friends with someone new and you want to invite them to hang out. What do you suggest doing?

    A. Go to a trendy new restaurant down the street
    B. Hang out at the park
    C. Open mic night at a club
    D. Mani/pedi or a sports activity

11. You're throwing a party. What does the invite say?

    A. "Grab a blanket for volleyball and s'mores on the beach."

    B. "Join us for a backyard BBQ and lawn games."

    C. "Wear your hottest dress for an all-night dance party."

    D. "Please come over for dinner and drinks."

12. You're in a room with others and the door falls off the hinges, your reaction is to...

    A. Put the door back up and fix it.

    B. Figure out why it fell off and make a plan to fix it.

    C. Say with excitement in your voice, "The door just fell off!"

    D. Find the maintenance guy so he can fix it. It looks horrible off the hinges!

Inbox Outbox Unbox NOBOX

13. How many pairs of shoes do you currently own?

    A. A lot, and I wear them all. They all have a purpose.
    B. A few, most are good quality, I usually get them on sale.
    C. You're joking, right? I don't have time to count them all.
    D. I have quite a few shoes. They are all organized and have a place in the closet.

Now that you have completed the shoe test, add up your answers and put your totals below.

A_____ B_____ C_____ D_____

Mostly A's = Sneakers

Your perfect shoes are sneakers, because you are an active individual. Whether you are using your shoes to do something active, or not, this style of shoe reflects your personality most accurately. In high school, you were the girl who was on a million different teams, and today you still strive to keep up an active lifestyle. You are hardworking, dedicated, and passionate about many things. You usually want your own way and like to be the driver of whatever you are doing. When you set your mind to something, you achieve it. You like to be challenged in life and thrive from taking on new experiences. More times than not, stress can be your motivator. You like to share adventures with others who share your passion for new challenges. After all your hard work though, you truly know how to enjoy life. Sneakers are usually risk takers.

Sneakers motto is: *"Work hard, play hard, and relax after achieving a goal."* You are down to earth, dedicated to yourself and others, and people are drawn to you because of your motivation and enthusiasm for life. You are social and tend to make friends easily. You are confident in your abilities. You also love to relax and slip on your flip flops to meet friends for something casual or to just hang out. When it comes to dressing up and going out on the town, you've got some sexy shoes in the back of the closet just for those occasions; but, the sneaker is your go-to shoe. With sneakers, you can hit the ground running. You tend to walk on your heels with decisiveness. You tend to be confident, ambitious, motivated, well-rounded, can be demanding, a pioneer to new adventures, a risk taker, a little sassy, decisive, and determined...these are just some characteristics that describe you. Your friends love your up-for-anything attitude—they just wish they had your energy.

"Keep calm...the shoes are under the bed!"

Sneakers movement is medium-high, and Yang Energy. Your element is fire. You never stay in the box for long. Sneakers know how to take-action, so getting out is easy. Your thinking process is compartmentalized, ambitious, expressive, and being demanding is vital for your success. Sneakers tend to be mostly extroverted.

"That awkward moment when
you are wearing your Nikes
and you can't do it."

"I like Cinderella—
she has a good work ethic
and she likes shoes."
—Amy Adams

What are the four steps sneakers should take to get NOBOX?

1. Trust your instincts.
2. As an extrovert, your Yang Energy allows you to look back, see the box where you've been, and to climb the walls to the highest mountains.
3. Don't overthink it. There are many solutions and more than one way to tie sneakers.
4. Sneakers are action-takers; so, sometimes they need to be told to slow down. Just as there are walking, jogging, and running shoes, you must pace yourself to NOBOX.

"It's always shoe o'clock somewhere."

"I like romantic walks in the shoe department."

Mostly B's = Flats/Loafers

Flats/Loafers are an intellectual, creative, and unique individual. The Flat/Loafer is your perfect shoe, because it's all about comfort and class. Sometimes you are totally casual and enjoy just a t-shirt and jeans, and at other times, you spice it up a bit with a skirt, a stylish top, and either a scarf or a hat. Either way, you look smart and distinct—both which represent you accurately. The loafer is an unpretentious shoe that fits your personality perfectly.

Let me make a distinction here: a loafer doesn't have to be the kind "old folks" wear. You know, the ones you put a penny in. Loafers include ballet flats, flats, moccasins, boat shoes, Tom's, and other stylish slip-ons.

You are a humble person who strives to portray yourself accurately. You can relate with people from all walks of life and you enjoy striking up conversations with total strangers. You enjoy hearing the stories of others and like to learn about new things and people constantly. You are an avid learner and enjoy discovering new music, art, travel destinations, and the best eateries. You have a knack for recognizing quality in things, such as: good food, wine, music, art, clothing, and craftsmanship. You are philosophical by nature, and enjoy stimulating conversation. You also truly enjoy creating things and others would describe you as innovative. Other attributes that describe you are: supportive, loyal, reliable, patient, kind, faithful, casual, unique, and intellect. That is you…you are a Flat/Loafer.

Flats/Loafers movement is low-medium and Yin Energy. Your element is water; so, you flow with ease and grace. Your thinking process is polished, mysterious, and flexible. Flats/Loafers are mostly introverted.

Flats/Loafers are careful when it comes to decision making, because it's comfortable and secure in the box. Life in the box is uncomplicated and reflects your inner energy.

"All I need is love…
NO new shoes!"

"You are either in your bed
or in your shoes…
it pays to invest in both."

What are the four steps Flats/Loafers should take to get NOBOX?

1. Get a plan…you need a plan.
2. Use your soft Yin fun-loving energies to experience and feel NOBOX.
3. You will need to stay connected to your nurturing nature if you transition to the NOBOX.
4. Stay grounded. Keep your whole foot on the ground just like the flat/loafer.

Inbox Outbox Unbox NOBOX

www.HollyPorter.com

Mostly C's = Boots

"Whose bed have your boots been under?"

"Eat the taco, the cowboy boots will still fit."

Inbox Outbox Unbox NOBOX

That's right! You are the boot! There are many different styles of boots; yet, they all bring us back to the same characteristics. You are a creative and diverse person, and that's why the boot fits you perfectly. You are cautious and precise. You are totally okay with dressing down and wearing jeans and a t-shirt; but, you also love to dress yourself up a bit and show off your unique sense of style. Boots are smart, tactful, down to earth, and curious. You love to learn about new things and challenge yourself in all areas of your life. You also love to relax and throw on a pair of flip flops or stylish sandals to meet friends for down time. Boots are all about the relationship. Others would describe you as hardworking, yet easy-going, open-minded, and free spirited. Boots are all about the fun they can have. You are always up for a new adventure and traveling is definitely a passion of yours.

You are a person of many hats. You don't fit into the box, and you love that about yourself. You are witty, sharp, clever, adventurous, and to the point. There is no false bone in your body. You are honest, unique, inquisitive, and strong...these are just some characteristics of your personality.

You enjoy taking on new adventures in life; whether it's traveling to a new city, meeting new people, and/or trying different hobbies and occupations. You thrive from a challenge and others know you as hardworking and as a fun and lively individual. You love life and don't think any minute of it should be wasted. Every moment is an opportunity, and you wholeheartedly intend to live it to the fullest! You are a little bit wild...and you are proud of it.

Inbox Outbox Unbox NOBOX

You have your act together and are always up for any challenge…just like a sturdy pair of boots. You also would never let someone walk all over you—or the people you love.

As far as movement is concerned, Boots are the highest of all the personalities. Your energy is Yang and your element is air. You breathe life into others and light up the room by entering it. Boots thinking process is bouncy, active, playful, spirited, vibrant, and friendly. Boots are, to no surprise, mostly extroverted!

"I don't need any more shoes…
Oh…look…new shoes!"
—Dory

"Stay calm
and steal everybody's left shoe."

What are the four steps Boots should take to get NOBOX?

1. Do the *Boot Scootin' Boogie* and use the spring in your step to dance all the way to NOBOX. Bring all your friends along…it must be fun for you.
2. Use your Yang Energy and charismatic way to shine and move towards the journey ahead. That silver-lining is always easy for you to see. Boots love the ride, so always remember to go in style.
3. Keep things simple. Don't make the thought of NOBOX too complicated.
4. Celebrate all along the way and trust yourself. The path may seem long, so make it magical!

"CHASE YOUR DREAMS…
in high heels of course."

"I can't help it if I'm a stiletto
in a world of Uggs."

Mostly D's = Heels

You are confident and sexy; therefore, the heel is the shoe for you. You are structured and live by your calendar. You love to be in charge and want everyone to have a good time at any event. Heels are nice and speak serious fashion and commitment to looking your best. You are sociable and outgoing with others; however, very proper about it. You know how to dress to impress and aren't afraid to show yourself off. You are comfortable with your fabulous self and others love this about you. You also enjoy relaxing and certainly love lounging around in you pj's to catch up on your favorite TV show.

You have days where you prefer to grab your flip-flops and go completely casual; but, the heel is your signature shoe. Other attributes of the Heel are: sexy,

47

confident, smart, clever, and sophisticated…yep, that's you! Heels are flirty and feminine. You prefer an environment that allows for consistency, dependability, and structure. You are most often seen as cool, calm, and collected on the outside (whether that is true on the inside or not).

You possess excellent listening skills—some of the best in fact. Heels possess an amazing ability to calm those who are upset. You're always willing to help in a pressure situation…even if you don't really want to.

Heels are striking; although, let's face it, you could turn heads in rubber flip-flops and a pair of overalls…it's just who you are. You are gorgeous, both inside and out.

Heels element is Earth, and your energy is Yin.

Your movement is the lowest of all personalities—it's precise (could be observed as almost still), and that makes Heels mostly introverted.

"I felt sorry for myself because
I had no shoes, until
I met a man who had no feet."

What are the four steps Heels should take to get NOBOX?

1. Realize that it may take a bit longer than others to move through the decision of getting to NOBOX. Be patient with yourself.

2. Listen to your inner voice. Use your Yin Energy to guide you in the direction of taking your first step. Then, when you're ready, you will know how to move forward.

3. As you move along your way to NOBOX, don't let others bully or push you. It is okay to be cautious, thorough, and precise...your plan is perfect for you.

4. When you look back and see NOBOX, know you've structured your plan for yourself, followed the rules, predicted, and captivated the outcome you wanted for yourself. Now, reward yourself.

www.HollyPorter.com

CONCLUSION

Now that you have experienced all the shoe persona's...was it fun, adventurous, realistic, and educational? Did you learn something new? If so (and I hope so), then I feel accomplished! My wish for you is that you now have a better idea as to whom you are and how you can do things differently in the future.

"No matter how much I eat,
the shoes still fit."

My final note to each of you:

Sneakers

Do you move through life so fast that you find yourself present in body, but not present in mind? If so, stop and smell the roses.

Flats/Loafers

Maybe you see that you need a little more fun in your life. Well then, spice it up! Perhaps, you realize you think about a situation more than you ought to. Well then, breathe. You don't need to analyze everything.

Boots

Because you are playful, and love to be around and involved with others, maybe you don't always "get the joke"...realize, you are smarter than others make you feel and your smile is contagious.

Heels

Is there so much structure, that you find it challenging to even think about coloring outside of the lines? Well then, grab some paint and get messy…you will be just fine.

Remember, there is much information out there for you to explore to get to know your personality style better. In this book, my desire is to give you a little information that can help you along your journey of life.

Before we part ways, I'd like to share a few secrets with you that were shared with me by several others. These are secrets that I have implemented into my life and that help me through each day.

"You're only one new pair of shoes away from a good mood."

15 Strategies Any Shoe Persona Can Do To Get Better Life Results.

1. Clean out the clutter in your life. Do what I call, "Clean House." Clean house with your home, your friends, and anything that is not in harmony with the direction you are headed. If it isn't serving you well, get rid of it!

2. Keep your desk and counters free of extra papers and "stuff." It is hard to focus when your surroundings are a mess. As my good friend, Elena, says, "Everything has a home." If there isn't a home for it, then you probably don't need it. If you don't have a system, find one or create one to help you

get organized.

3. Speaking of systems, if you put some into place, your life and business will run much more efficient...which means you will accomplish more with less stress. Keep a task list of things you must accomplish and number them in order of importance.

4. You can use the 3D-system. Do it, Delegate it, or Delete it. This system gives you three choices of what to do every day to remove tasks off your list. By the end of each day, the list is gone; because, you did it, delegated it to someone else, or you deleted it—either permanently or for the day. Create a filing system with a folder for each day of

the week. Organize each task for each day into two categories: 1. Trivial Many 2. Critical Few. The Trivial Many tasks are all the things you do in your day that really don't matter as much; but, they make you feel like you have crossed off a lot on your to-do list. Critical few, are the tasks that are most important—ranking the highest priority— but, they usually take the longest and aren't as fun to do. Your goal is to put the Critical Few first on your list and get them over with. Be careful not to sabotage your own success. Make a list that is doable.

5. Outsource. You cannot be everything to everyone; so, delegate tasks to those who have more expertise than you. (Enlace, Fivver, Odesk, Freelancer, or

local college students are great for this.) Once you begin to delegate tasks, you can spend more time in your genius zone and on your MMAs (Money Making Activities).

6. Separate personal and business time. I know, I know, with technology making it easy to work while you play (especially for those who have a laptop lifestyle), you still need time to wind down and do some self-care.

7. Which now brings me to self-care. (This should probably have been #1 on this list.) If you don't take care of you, you are not going to be great for anyone else! Maybe it's something simple, like a bubble bath, a walk in the park, dinner with friends,

or reading this book…figure out what self-care looks like for you and make sure you do plenty of it!

8. Quiet your mind. Do this by allowing yourself to have some thinking time and private time. One idea for you to implement is to put a STOP sign on your door for others to see and know that you are currently unavailable. Make sure your phone is on vibrate…or, better yet, off. During this time, take a few minutes to breathe, meditate, or catch a power nap. Once you are refreshed and ready to be accessible to others again, be sure to turn your phone back on to normal settings.

9. Strive to focus on one project at a time. It is too easy today to multitask. Funny thing is, we tend to believe that we are good at it. STOP! It is just confusing your mind. If you are like me and find yourself saying "focus, focus, focus" all the time, then you know it is time to slow down, stop multitasking, and take a break!

10. Do periodic self-check-ins. Ask yourself questions like: Am I using my time wisely? Could I do this different? Is there a better way to get this done?

11. Have boundaries. In a world of, *quick and easy,* and, *immediate gratification,* set boundaries for all who pull at your coattail. Remember, it is okay for people to wait. Don't feel the need to always have

to respond immediately to others. Have a set time when you will be on social media, check your emails, and return phone calls. Otherwise, others will highjack your time, and before you know it, the day is over!

12. Schedule work (or those Critical Few tasks), during your prime time—the time of day when you tend to accomplish the most and are the most productive. (My prime time is 10am-2pm.) I often jokingly tell my husband, "Sorry you missed it!"

13. Take breaks throughout the day. Walk around a little, stretch your legs, go up and down some stairs, and stay hydrated. Taking much needed

breaks during the day will increase your focus and productivity.

14. Set alarms for meetings and tasks that you don't want to forget. This way you are not looking at the clock all day, wondering if "it's time" for something. Make sure it's a different ring tone than everything else, so it is sure to capture your attention.

15. Create a reward system for yourself. (Whatever that looks like for you.) Celebrate life and everything you accomplish. You deserve it after all!

The Author

Holly Porter

"Chocolate is good,
but shoes are carb free."

"Life is too short
to wear boring shoes."

68

"Do not judge my path.
You haven't walked in my shoes
or ridden my broom."

"It takes a strong woman to admit
she has enough shoes,
which I totally don't."

"Dear Santa, I've been naughty,
I'd like some shoes to match."

"The only thing I love
more than shoes
is a closetful."